ELEVATE

Mindset Matters Athletics
Mental Performance Playbook

DAN DAVIS AND CHAD DENNIS

WESTBOW
P R E S S®
A DIVISION OF THOMAS NELSON
& ZONDERVAN

WestBow Press books may be ordered through booksellers or by contacting:

WestBow Press
A Division of Thomas Nelson & Zondervan
1663 Liberty Drive
Bloomington, IN 47403
www.westbowpress.com
844-714-3454

ISBN: 979-8-3850-1696-9 (sc)
ISBN: 979-8-3850-1697-6 (e)

Library of Congress Control Number: 2024900767

Print information available on the last page.

WestBow Press rev. date: 02/20/2024

CONTENTS

Introduction.. vii

Camp 1 Elevated Mindset 1
Camp 2 Line Of Action... 8
Camp 3 Extreme Ownership 17
Camp 4 Visualization... 24
Camp 5 Attitude 30
Camp 6 Train... 37
Camp 7 Evaluate 45

Conclusion 51
Acknowledgments 53
Bibliography...55
About the Coaches 57

INTRODUCTION

ELEVATE

Welcome to Mindset Matters Athletics and our E.L.E.V.A.T.E program! You are in the right place if you want to take your athletic game to the next level, mentally and physically.

Sports have always been a big part of my life, and I'm sure they're a big part of yours, too. But have you ever thought about the valuable life lessons that come along with being an athlete? Whether you realize it or not, athletics provides a fantastic opportunity to impact your life and those around you positively. That's why sports are such a big deal in almost every culture. Thousands of years ago, people would gather to challenge each other and determine who was the fastest, the strongest, or the toughest.

The competition between athletes creates impressive energy, passion, and entertainment. It also allows individuals and communities to unite and support their favorite athlete or team. But more than that, sports develop bonds, friendships, and rivalries long after the game ends.

As athletes, we constantly push ourselves to be our best. And that's precisely what the Elevate Playbook is designed to help us do. Whether you're looking to become a pro athlete or just want to improve your overall performance and mindset, this program will give you the tools and strategies you need to succeed both on and off the field. Through this program, we'll explore various aspects of our Elevate Program and uncover techniques to enhance your mental resilience, boost your physical capabilities, and foster a winning mindset. We'll discuss the importance of goal setting, visualization, self-discipline, and teamwork. Along the way, you'll learn from the experiences and insights of successful athletes and coaches who have mastered the art of elevating their game.

Are you ready to take your athletic game to the next level? To unleash your full potential, overcome obstacles, and achieve greatness? It's time to E.L.E.V.A.T.E. As athletes, we strive for excellence both on and off the field. In my opinion, that's the true power of sports. They can transform individual lives and entire communities, making the world better. And that's where Mindset Matters Athletics comes in. We're dedicated to making a positive impact on everyone around us.

We firmly believe that sports translate directly to life itself. Sports and athletics have a profound impact beyond determining who's better on a given day or who wins and loses. They shape the trajectory of our lives and prepare us to face life's challenges. And here's the thing: you'll be competing for the rest of your life, whether for a job, a spouse, or a promotion. Life cannot be lived without a willingness to compete. Sports teach us this valuable skill and show us that failure is not the end. When we fail, we regroup, prepare a plan of action, and get back in the game. Failure is simply a stepping stone to success.

Life can be challenging, and we know that everyone reading this has faced their challenges and obstacles. But we want you to know that you're not alone. With the right mindset and support, you can overcome anything. At Mindset Matters Athletics, we believe in physically, mentally, and emotionally becoming the best version of ourselves. We're here to help you do just that.

So, are you ready to start your transformation? To become the best version of yourself and live the life you've always dreamed of? Let's do this! We've got you covered if you're an athlete looking to elevate your performance on and off the field. Our coaches have put in a lot of effort to create an incredible mental performance training program to help you develop skills, strategies, and tactics to improve your performance in sports and life.

Our coaches have a wealth of experience in sports, having played and coached at the highest levels. They also have real-life experience in Military Special Operations, Public Safety Service, SWAT operations, Leadership, and education, which gives them a unique perspective on what it takes to succeed. The path to success is not easy, but it's simple. It involves understanding the Elite Mindset, learning the power of proper discipline, and understanding how processes and systems impact outcomes. These things separate the best from the rest, the successful from the unsuccessful.

Our most valuable asset is time, and it's running out. It's up to us how we use it, and we want to help you use it effectively. Once it's gone, it's gone, so we need to use it wisely. The sooner you start doing the hard things required to become a champion and discipline yourself to stay focused on your goals, the sooner you'll reach your potential and achieve true freedom!

Our program, Elevate, is designed to help you get there. We named it Elevate because if you follow our program and implement the skills, strategies, and tactics into your everyday life, the sky's the limit. The program consists of seven stages or camps, each focusing on mental performance training.

Camp #1 focuses on developing an Elevated Mindset understanding it is a choice.

Camp #2 helps you master the Line of Action and establish clear goals.

Camp #3 is about extreme ownership and developing self-control and discipline.

Camp #4 teaches you the power of Visualization because you have to see it to be it.

Camp #5 focuses on Attitude and the power of positivity.

Camp #6 helps you Train habits and routines of excellence.

Camp #7 teaches you to Evaluate everything and manage your time effectively.

At Mindset Matters Athletics, our mission is to create a movement of success-minded, mentally tough, disciplined, resilient athletes who will positively impact the world. If that sounds like something you're interested in, look at our Elevate program and see how it can help you reach your goals!

Our approach goes beyond sports and focuses on transforming lives. We believe serving others and positively impacting those around us is crucial to personal growth and success. We understand that sports and life are not solitary journeys; we rely on others to help us reach our goals. As athletes, fostering a culture of growth and development by supporting and learning from successful teammates is essential. Competition helps us build resilience and strengthens our resolve. Regardless of our challenges, we never give up and embrace them head-on. We strive to improve our performance in all areas of life, knowing that excellence in multiple aspects directly translates to success on the field, court, or any other arena.

Above all, we expect success. Our focus is building confident, strong, and positive-minded individuals equipped to make a difference in their communities. We emphasize thorough preparation, leaving no doubt that we have done everything possible to position ourselves for success. As Brian Cain aptly said, "Don't count the days; make the days count." We encourage athletes to seize each day as an opportunity to challenge themselves, strive to be their best, and expect greatness.

MINDSET MATTERS ATHLETICS

E — ELITE MINDEST

An elite mindset forms the bedrock upon which success is built. By understanding its significance, evaluating our current mindset, and implementing strategies for improvement, we can train our minds to reach an elite level. This transformation opens the door to an elevated perspective and ultimately paves the way for elite performance in all areas of life.

L — LINE OF ACTION

Every athlete with an elite mindset relentlessly pursues greatness. However, it is the establishment of a well-defined process that gives direction to this pursuit, laying the groundwork for success. While outcomes hold significance, fixating solely on winning and results can be detrimental. The sheer number of uncontrollable variables in sports necessitates a focus on what we can control—the process

E — EXTREME OWNERSHIP

Extreme Ownership is a mindset and approach that emphasizes taking complete responsibility for one's actions, decisions, and outcomes in life. It involves setting aside ego, making no excuses, and fully owning both successes and failures. This mindset is essential for personal growth, overcoming adversity, improving resiliency and achieving one's goals.

V — VISUALIZATION

Through visualization, we gain mental repetitions in a controlled environment, where we have the liberty to choose every scenario and situation simply by imagining them unfolding in real-time, right at this very moment. It is an opportunity for us to tap into the most complex, intelligent, and dynamic organ on the planet—our brain.

A — ATTITUDE

By cultivating a positive attitude, we open ourselves up to new possibilities, attract positive experiences, and create a supportive environment for success. It'simportant to remember that our attitude is a choice, and by choosing positivity and gratitude, we can transform our lives and make a positive impact on others.

T — TRAIN

The significance of habits cannot be underestimated. Our daily actions, weekly routines, monthly commitments, and yearly consistency shape us. Whether we reach our full potential or fall short is directly influenced by our habits. It is the accumulation of small actions performed consistently over time that yields substantial results, rather than sporadic bursts of motivation.

E — EVALUATE

Continuously assess your 14.24 and 168. Remember that 14 minutes and 24 seconds make up 1% of our day. Are you intentional about utilizing that time to improve yourself each day? Plan how you will use your 14.24 to get better. Similarly, review and evaluate your 168 schedule.Have you been intentional about your time or allowed others to dictate it? Guard your schedule,as time is your most precious resource.

ELEVATE handout

ELEVATED MINDSET

An example of an elevated (growth/elite) mindset in sports for athletes is when they believe that their abilities and performance can be improved with hard work and dedication. For instance, a basketball player with a growth mindset may miss a shot during a game. Still, instead of getting discouraged, they might use it to focus on improving their form and technique. They might practice shooting from different angles, work on their footwork, and analyze their game footage to identify areas for improvement. Adopting a growth mindset makes athletes more likely to stay motivated and continue improving their skills, leading to better performance on the court.

According to a study published in the Journal of Applied Sport Psychology, "Elite athletes tend to possess an elite mindset characterized by a strong sense of purpose, high levels of self-discipline, and an unrelenting drive to succeed." (Gould, D., Dieffenbach, K., & Moffett, A. (2002).

Indeed, having an elite mindset serves as the ultimate foundation for success for athletes. It sets the tone for their decisions and actions, yet many fail to understand or underestimate its power. At Mindset Matters Athletics, we believe it is crucial to outline our definition of an elite mindset and emphasize why possessing one is vital for success in sports.

To begin, we will establish the groundwork by defining what we mean by an elite mindset. At its core, an elite mindset refers to a state of thinking that surpasses the norm and sets athletes apart. It encompasses superior abilities, qualities, and perspectives compared to the larger group or society.

By comprehending the definitions of "elite" and "mindset," athletes can recognize the tremendous power of creating an elite mindset. This mindset serves as the flame that ignites an elite perspective. When they adopt an elite perspective, they perceive challenges as opportunities and setbacks as feedback for growth. It is from this vantage point that elite performance emerges.

An elite mindset forms the foundation for success in sports for athletes. By understanding its significance, evaluating their current mindset, and implementing strategies for improvement, they can train their minds to reach an elite level. This transformation opens the door to an elevated perspective and ultimately paves the way for elite performance in their sport.

As an athlete, you know that embracing an elite mindset lies in your hands. Are you ready to become a victor rather than a victim? Let's look at the stories of successful athletes like Corbin Burnes, the 2021 Cy Young award winner, who transformed their mindset and achieved extraordinary success. Becoming the 2021 National League Cy Young Award winner demonstrates his development of an elite perspective. By working on his mental game, he overcame challenges and reached a higher level of performance.

Now, let's talk about some of the most successful athletes of our time. Tom Brady's success can be attributed to his ability to control his emotions, adapt his playing style, and surround himself with high-value teammates. His focus on work-life balance and his relentless drive to win exemplifies his elite mindset. Similarly, Kobe Bryant was known for his fierce competitiveness and unwavering commitment to excellence. His willingness to be coached and dedication to improvement highlights his elite mindset.

One inspiring story of an athlete who changed their mindset and achieved greatness is that of Michael Jordan, widely regarded as one of the greatest basketball players ever. Despite his natural talent and early success in basketball, Jordan faced a setback early in his career when his team, the Chicago Bulls, was consistently defeated by their rivals, the Detroit Pistons. Jordan struggled to overcome this obstacle, often feeling frustrated and defeated after each loss. However, after some reflection and self-evaluation, Jordan realized he needed to change his mindset to achieve greatness. He focused less on individual success and more on elevating his team's performance. He also worked tirelessly to improve his physical and mental preparation, dedicating himself to a rigorous training regimen and adopting a more disciplined lifestyle. The results were remarkable.

Jordan led the Bulls to six N.B.A. championships and was named the league's Most Valuable Player five times. He also became known for his clutch performances in high-pressure situations, earning the nickname "Air Jordan" for his spectacular dunks and game-winning shots. Jordan's story is a testament to the power of mindset and the importance of hard work and dedication in achieving greatness. By changing his mindset and working to improve his skills and discipline, he overcame obstacles and achieved unparalleled success in his sport.

As an athlete, you can learn a lot from these successful athletes. They exemplify characteristics of an elite mindset, such as perseverance, dedication, a growth-oriented perspective, and a relentless pursuit of improvement and excellence. Their mental approach and attitude played a significant role in their exceptional achievements.

The entire premise of mental performance can be based on faith. One scripture verse that emphasizes the importance of a process over outcome mentality is Colossians 3:23-24: "Whatever you do, work at it with all your heart, as working for the Lord, not for human masters, since you know that you will receive an inheritance from the Lord as a reward. It is the Lord Christ you are serving." This passage encourages us to focus on doing our best in everything we do, regardless of the outcome or the recognition we may receive from others. It reminds us that, ultimately, we are serving God and working for His glory and that our efforts will be rewarded in His kingdom. This verse emphasizes that we should focus on doing our best and working diligently rather than becoming overly fixated on achieving a specific outcome. It reminds us that our efforts and attitude are just as significant as the result and that we should strive to honor God in all we do.

Remember to stay focused, embrace self-evaluation, and train your brain to dominate your game. The journey towards an elite mindset is ongoing, and by consistently implementing strategies and seeking growth, you can continue to progress and enhance your mental performance.

THERE ARE TWO MINDSETS:

AVERAGE MINDSET VS ELEVATED MINDSET

AVERAGE MINDSET	ELEVATED MINDSET
MAKES EXCUSES	MAKES IT HAPPEN
CONFIDENCE IS A FEELING	CONFIDENCE IS AN ACTION
FOCUSES ON WHAT THEY CAN'T CONTROL	FOCUSES ON WHAT THEY CAN CONTROL
AVOIDS CHALLENGES	EMBRACES CHALLENGES
SEES FAILURE AS FINAL	SEES FAILURE AS POSITIVE FEEDBACK
SEES OTHER'S SUCCESS AS A THREAT OR SOURCE OF JEALOUSY	SEES OTHER'S SUCCESS AS A SOURCE OF INSPIRATION

What mindset do you have?
E.L.E.V.A.T.E. your mindset!

visit: www.mindsetmattersathletics.com or e-mail: info@mindsetmattersathletics.com

Average v elevated mindset

MMA BFS Worksheet (Self Awareness)

MINDSET MATTERS ATHLETICS

Please list in as much detail as possible what it is like for you when you are at your best versus when you struggle in performance with your body language, focus, and self-talk.

	At my best		When I struggle
Body Language			
Focus			
Self-Talk			

BFS worksheet

FIELD NOTES

Elevated Mindset

- Foundation of Mental Performance
- Founded in "Purpose" of "Why"
- Requires a Decision and Disciplne
- Is the Foundation of Success
- Generates Greater Perserverance and Higher Levels of Relentlessness
- Creates Exponential Growth

CAMP
TWO

LINE OF ACTION

Coach Dennis

In sports, goal development is crucial for athletes, and setting SMART goals (specific, measurable, achievable, relevant, and time-bound) is a great way to achieve that. For instance, a long-distance runner may aim to improve their time for a 10K race. They can set a specific goal, such as running a race in under 45 minutes, measure their progress by tracking the time using a stopwatch or fitness tracking app, make it achievable by gradually increasing their training and setting milestones along the way, make it relevant to their overall fitness and competitive goals, and time-bound by setting a deadline for the race. By setting SMART goals, athletes can stay motivated and focused and track their progress toward achieving their desired outcome.

One study published in the Journal of Sport and Exercise Psychology examined the impact of goal-setting on the performance of collegiate swimmers. The study found that swimmers who set specific, challenging goals performed significantly better than those who did not set goals or set vague, non-specific goals. The study also found that swimmers who received feedback on their progress toward their goals performed even better than those who simply set goals without feedback. Overall, the study highlights the power of goal development in athletics and suggests that setting specific and challenging goals and receiving feedback on progress can lead to improved performance. (Kleiber, D. A., & Brock, S. J. (1992)

At Mindset Matters Athletics, we understand the intricacies of athletic performance and how to execute a program effectively. We believe in the principle of "process over outcome" as the cornerstone of our training approach, both mentally and physically. Every athlete with an elite mindset relentlessly pursues greatness. Still, it is the establishment of a well-defined process that gives direction to this pursuit and lays the groundwork for success.

While outcomes hold significance, fixating solely on winning and results can be detrimental. There are many uncontrollable variables in sports, so it is essential to focus on what athletes can control—the process. By staying balanced and centered, athletes can allow their minds to calculate and react rationally to any situation or obstacle.

Maintaining composure during high-stakes moments is a hallmark of elite athletes. The ability to remain unflappable, commonly referred to as having "ice in their veins," stems from their mastery of controlling the chaos. These athletes execute their meticulously crafted process, leveraging self-awareness to make necessary adjustments and exhibiting immense self-discipline. They remain present, unaffected by external pressures, enabling them to deliver exceptional performances when it matters most.

At Mindset Matters Athletics, we use the Intentional Goal Development (I.G.D.) system, designed specifically for athletes, to drive goal achievement. Intentionality permeates every aspect of our training regimens, team coaching, and individual mentorship. Setting goals becomes a strategic and intentional process with the I.G.D. system.

We start by formulating SMART goals that are Specific, Measurable, Achievable, Relevant, and Time-bound. These goals are written down, giving them tangible existence and empowering athletes to visualize their accomplishments as they have already transpired. However, remaining connected to the underlying motivation—the "why" behind the goals is crucial. The unyielding desire to overcome obstacles fuels the drive to push past moments of doubt and adversity.

Vividly envisioning the attainment of goals is crucial for athletes. They can immerse themselves in the future they seek by visualizing themselves succeeding in their sport, achieving their personal best, and reaching their ultimate aspirations. By meticulously visualizing their ideal selves, athletes can chart a course toward their envisioned future and bridge the gap between their present abilities and ultimate ambitions.

During goal setting, individuals pursuing their athletic aspirations identify the actionable steps necessary for progress. Some actions may be readily apparent—such as doubling down on academic efforts or engaging in focused physical training. Others may require reaching out to potential schools, networking with industry professionals, or working closely with a mental performance coach to cultivate resilience and mental fortitude.

These action steps are meticulously detailed, serving as a roadmap to success.

Individuals pursuing their athletic aspirations understand that while guidance and mentorship play a vital role, the onus lies on their shoulders to execute the plan. Ownership and personal responsibility are paramount. The indomitable spirit to achieve resides within each one of us; through our unwavering dedication, persistence, and unwavering commitment, we can make our goals a reality.

Executing the plan demands sacrifice and tough decision-making. Individuals prioritize their goals, making choices that align with their aspirations and dedicating themselves fully to the journey. Success is a culmination of consistent, unwavering effort, and individuals celebrate each milestone reached along the way, fueling their momentum and reinforcing their belief in the process.

Line of Action equips individuals with the tools, mindset, and game plan to excel. By embracing the process, visualizing success, and taking intentional action, they can unlock their full potential and embark on a transformative journey toward athletic greatness. As Brian Cain famously preaches, "Do a little a lot, not a lot a little, and you'll achieve monumental results!" This principle holds not only in athletics but also in the pursuit of personal excellence. Let's dive deeper into these strategies and apply them to your goals, unleashing your athletic prowess.

If you yearn to enhance your physical prowess (Telescopic Goal), unleash your inner athlete by conquering a daily lap around campus. It may appear as a mere stride, but it is a stepping stone to greatness. Embrace the grind and let each decisive step propel you toward peak fitness. Likewise, if your ambition is to read 25 books (Telescopic Goal), ignite your mental stamina by consuming the pages for five minutes each night before surrendering to slumber (Microscopic Goal). Harness that intensity and witness how consistent dedication to this routine fortifies your literary muscles.

Now, the keys to triumphantly conquering your goals await your grasp! Stay unwaveringly focused on your "why." It shall be the inferno fueling your relentless drive. This process is simple, but don't be fooled—it's a grueling ascent. We must pinpoint our starting line and keep our sights firmly affixed to our desired destination. Brace yourself for the grueling test that lies ahead. Some days, you won't feel the fire blazing within, but remember, the most extraordinary accomplishments stem from surpassing these adversities. Visualize success with crystalline clarity, for it fuels the furnace of unwavering determination. Retain a laser-like focus on the process and let your dreams soar.

You know that action spawns energy as an athlete, so dream big and act with audacity. Tread fearlessly, for it is your path to unprecedented growth. While outcomes tantalize the mind, the minuit daily actions sculpt the champion within.

Embrace the philosophy of the next 200 feet—a span akin to the illuminated stretch cast by a car's headlights. You dismantle the grandest aspirations into digestible milestones by devoutly concentrating on each fleeting segment. Believe in the process, relish the expedition, and glory in the remarkable transformation it begets.

Motivation is the electrifying surge, the forceful shove that propels you into action. As Brian Cain wisely states, "It's the start that stops most people." To overcome that initial hurdle, tap into the wellspring of your motivation. Unearth your "why" with utmost clarity, for it is the catalyst that ignites the flames of determination and propels you on your journey.

Conversely, commitment is the lifeblood, fueling your relentless pursuit and endowing you with the unwavering energy to conquer even the steepest mountains. It demands grit—an unyielding spirit encapsulated by the acronym "Get Ready It's Tough." Research suggests that grit is the most significant predictor of success we can nurture. It is the reservoir of drive, resilience, and refusal to surrender. It requires no inherent talent, strength, or skill. Instead, it hinges on the unwavering belief that you will persevere and triumph despite obstacles.

One inspiring story of an athlete who used goals to get to where they wanted to be in sports is that of Mia Hamm, one of the greatest female soccer players ever. As a young girl, Hamm dreamed of playing for the U.S. national soccer team and winning an Olympic gold medal. To achieve these goals, she set a series of smaller, achievable goals to help her get closer to her ultimate objectives.

For example, one of her early goals was to become the

top scorer on her youth soccer team. She worked tirelessly to improve her fitness skills, practicing for hours daily and studying the game to learn new strategies and techniques. She achieved this goal with hard work and dedication and became a star player for her high school and college teams. Hamm continued to set and achieve goals throughout her career, including becoming the youngest player ever to join the U.S. national team at age 15, winning two World Cup championships and two Olympic gold medals, and being named FIFA's World Player of the Year twice. Hamm's story is a testament to the power of goal setting and the importance of hard work and dedication in achieving success in sports. By setting clear, achievable goals and working tirelessly to achieve them, she overcame obstacles and fulfilled her dreams. (Hamm, M., & Heifetz, A. (2000).

You may ask why motivation, commitment, and grit are paramount. As an athlete, you know there will be days when human nature beckons us to stray from the arduous path leading to our goals. You may be burdened by the trials of a challenging day at practice, conflicts with your teammates, or the stern rebukes of a demanding coach. Perhaps you seek respite from the fatigue that follows intense training sessions. It could be the weight of injuries, stress, or relationship turmoil. On these trying days, when the work seems arduous, motivation and commitment emerge as our guiding beacons, leading us toward our goals. That is precisely why understanding your "why" holds such tremendous significance. Your "why" towers above fleeting emotions, wielding the power to override momentary disinclinations. To gauge your commitment, delve deep into introspection and pose questions.

Write your mission statement by filling in the blanks to the sentence below:

I am achieving (write goal here)
_____this season because (write benefits here), _____and I know that the costs of achieving this goal are (Write costs here)
_____Which I accept because I am on a mission to become the most successful/best version of myself.

Your answer
....

MMA mission statement

FIELD NOTES

Line of Action

- SMART Goals (Specific, Measurable, Achievable, Relevant and Time Bound)
- I.G.D. (Intentional Goal Development)
- Requires Complete Clarity and Direction (Understand where you are and where you want to go!)
- Requires Intentional Execution of the Process
- Focuses on the Process over Outcome

CAMP
THREE

EXTREME OWNERSHIP

MMA Athlete Wrestler with Coach Davis

An example of extreme ownership in sports is when athletes take full responsibility for their performance and outcomes, regardless of external factors. For instance, a soccer player who loses a game may identify areas where they could have improved their performance instead of blaming the referee, weather conditions, or other external factors. They may review game footage, analyze their tactics, and identify areas for improvement in their training and strategy. By taking extreme ownership, athletes can develop a culture of accountability, resilience, and continuous improvement, leading to better performance and outcomes in the long run.

A study published in the Journal of Human Kinetics found that "Extreme ownership, or taking complete responsibility for one's actions and outcomes, is a key factor in the success of elite athletes. Athletes who exhibit extreme ownership are likelier to take initiative, persevere through challenges, and maintain a positive mindset in adversity." (Tod, D., Thatcher, R., & Rahman, R. (2015).

Extreme ownership is a mindset and approach emphasizing taking complete responsibility for one's actions, decisions, and outcomes in sports and life. It involves setting aside ego, making no excuses, and fully owning successes and failures. This mindset is essential for personal growth, overcoming adversity, and achieving goals. To build Extreme Ownership, several strategies can be employed:

Adjust your thinking: Adopt an extreme ownership mindset in your thoughts and actions. Commit to owning everything in your sports career and approach challenges with high intensity, commitment, and focus. Failure should not be an option, and even if you fall short, strive for tremendous improvement and raise performance levels.

Personal Vision Statement: Write down who you are as an athlete, why you want what you want, and what success looks like. Be extremely clear and honest in this process. Identify what you will tolerate and won't, the people you want in your sports career, and those who may need to be removed if they hold you back.

Own Your Failures and Setbacks: Acknowledge and

accept your mistakes and failures. Avoid hiding from them, pointing fingers, or making excuses. Instead, learn from them, adjust, and return to the game quickly. Remember that mistakes are a natural part of growth and should be made while striving to make something positive happen.

Be Coachable: Embrace the idea that everyone needs coaching and be open to feedback and guidance from mentors, coaches, and teammates. Seek out those who can provide honest and constructive criticism, challenge you, and help you improve. Being coachable is a sign of an elite mindset and extreme ownership. By embracing Extreme Ownership, several benefits can be obtained:

Increased Responsibility: Extreme Ownership makes athletes more responsible for their actions, behaviors, and goals. Taking personal responsibility allows coaches and teammates to trust and be inspired by you. It is critical for individual success both on and off the field.

Less Conflicts and Building Trust: Extreme Ownership reduces conflicts by eliminating the blame game. When athletes own their mistakes and take responsibility, conflicts are minimized, and trust is built among teammates. This trust becomes the glue that holds teams and players together.

Improved Performance: Extreme Ownership leads to explosive growth in performance. By taking responsibility, seeking feedback, and using setbacks as fuel for improvement, athletes can enhance their performance and reach higher levels of excellence.

Inspired Confidence: Extreme Ownership builds confidence as athletes realize how far they have come and acknowledge the hard work they have put in. Confidence grows because they know they can handle anything that comes their way. By owning everything, failure is not seen as final but as feedback that allows continuous improvement.

Athletes who embrace Extreme Ownership take full responsibility for their performance and outcomes. This mindset frees them to try new things, push their limits, and explore new possibilities without being held back by self-doubt or fear of failure. Extreme ownership requires a deep level of commitment, discipline, and self-reflection. Athletes who adopt this mindset take ownership of every aspect of their training and competition, including their successes and failures.

To build extreme ownership, athletes must be willing to make sacrifices and be "all in" to achieve their goals. This may involve stepping outside their comfort zone, making difficult decisions, and putting in the necessary work and effort.

Athletes can adjust their thinking by elevating their thoughts and actions to a higher intensity, commitment, and focus level. Failure should not be seen as an option but an opportunity for growth and improvement. They should set their intentions high; they will progress significantly despite falling short.

Owning failures and setbacks is crucial in building extreme ownership. It means accepting mistakes and taking responsibility for them. By owning their failures, athletes build trust with others and demonstrate resilience. Mistakes are viewed as learning opportunities, and they quickly adjust and get back in the game. When they realize that mistakes are not as big of a deal as they seem, they can stay focused on their process and continue to perform at a high level.

The Bible does not use the term "extreme ownership."

Still, several passages teach the importance of responsibility for actions and decisions. For example, Galatians 6:5 teaches us about personal responsibility and accountability. The passage reads: "For each will have to bear his load." This verse emphasizes that everyone is responsible for their actions and the consequences of those actions. In the context of the larger passage, Galatians 6:1-10, the author encourages believers to care for one another and help each other through difficult times. However, he also emphasizes that each person is ultimately responsible for their actions and should not rely solely on others to bear their burdens. The verse reminds us that we cannot blame others for our failures or mistakes or rely on others to carry us through life. Instead, we must take responsibility for our lives and actions and work towards our growth and development. Doing so can make us more responsible and better equipped to help others.

The benefits of extreme ownership for athletes are numerous. It makes them more responsible as they own their actions and behaviors. This leads to increased trust from coaches, teammates, and fans and the ability to inspire greatness in those around them. Extreme ownership also improves performance as athletes push themselves to new levels of growth and development. It boosts confidence as athletes recognize their abilities and become more willing to try new things and overcome obstacles. Ultimately, extreme ownership frees athletes to pursue their goals and aspirations relentlessly.

CAN CONTROL	CAN'T CONTROL

You must focus on what you can control

Control what you can control MMA worksheet

FIELD NOTES

Extreme Ownership

- Key Factor to Success in all Aspects of your Life
- Eliminate Excuses
- Allows Ownership of Setbacks and Failures to be used as Building Blocks of Resieliency
- Creates a Perspective where Failure is looked at as a Challenge and an Opportunity to get Better!
- Allows Individuals to become more Coachable
- Increases Responsibility, Trust and Improves Culture
- Improves Performance
- Generates Confidence

CAMP
FOUR

VISUALIZATION

MMA Athlete Fastpitch

An example of visualization in sports is when an athlete uses mental imagery to prepare for a competition or performance. For instance, a figure skater may visualize themselves performing their routine flawlessly from start to finish. They may imagine the feel of the ice beneath their blades, the sound of the music, and the crowd's applause. By visualizing the routine in detail, the athlete can create a mental blueprint for their performance, improving their confidence, focus, and muscle memory. Visualization can also help athletes prepare for unexpected challenges or setbacks by mentally rehearsing how they will respond and adapt to different situations.

A scientific study published in the Journal of Imagery Research in Sport and Physical Activity shows that visualization can improve athletic performance. The study found that when athletes engaged in mental imagery, they enhanced their skills, increased confidence, and reduced anxiety. The researchers also found that visualization was most effective when athletes combined it with physical practice, suggesting that visualization can supplement traditional training methods. Overall, the study indicates that visualization has the potential to be a powerful tool for athletes looking to improve their performance.

Visualization is a mental technique athletes use to prepare themselves for competitions or performances. It involves creating vivid images of the desired outcome to improve confidence, focus, and muscle memory. Athletes can use visualization to mentally rehearse their performances in detail, including the feel of the environment, the sound of the music, and the crowd's reaction. This helps them create a mental blueprint for their performance, enabling them to visualize themselves performing at their best.

Visualization can also help athletes prepare for unexpected challenges or setbacks by mentally rehearsing how they will respond and adapt to different situations. Despite its potential for explosive growth, visualization is often overlooked and underutilized in mental performance training. At Mindset Matters Athletics, we define visualization as the ability to construct mental simulations that closely resemble real-life situations. Our brains cannot discern between fantasy and reality, making visualization a powerful training tool. It allows us to engage in mental repetitions in a controlled environment, where we can choose every scenario and situation simply by imagining them unfolding in real-time. This enables us to tap into the planet's most complex, intelligent, and dynamic organ - our brain.

Visualization is a powerful tool that can help athletes remain calm and focused during tense situations. It involves imagining and experiencing scenarios in your mind before they physically manifest, enabling you to perform at your peak level. By employing visualization, you can manage stress, respond with logic, and easily navigate the ups and downs of competition.

Many professional athletes and teams use visualization training as a crucial component of their mental performance regimen due to its proven benefits on physical and psychological health. It can help you improve your performance, unlock your full potential, and enhance your mental well-being.

Phil Jackson, one of the most successful coaches in N.B.A. history, is known for his unique coaching style, emphasizing mental performance and mindfulness. His interest heavily influences Jackson's coaching philosophy in Zen Buddhism and Native American spirituality, and he often incorporates meditation and visualization techniques into his coaching. One of the critical aspects of Jackson's coaching style is his focus on developing a solid team culture built on trust, communication, and selflessness.

He also emphasizes the importance of mental

preparation and visualization, encouraging his players to use visualization techniques to rehearse their performance mentally and to stay focused and positive during games. Another important aspect of Jackson's coaching philosophy is his emphasis on mindfulness and present-moment awareness. He encourages his players to remain focused on the present moment and avoid being distracted by past mistakes or future worries. He also enables them to be open-minded and to approach challenges with a positive, growth-oriented mindset. Jackson's coaching style has been credited with helping his teams achieve remarkable success, including 11 N.B.A. championships with the Chicago Bulls and Los Angeles Lakers. His emphasis on mental performance and mindfulness has influenced sports psychology, and many coaches and athletes have adopted his techniques and philosophy to improve their performance.

The legendary Michael Jordan himself shared his perspective on visualization, stating that it helps slow things down and make them seem familiar. He used visualization to conquer his fear of failure and become a basketball master.

You can employ various methods and techniques to incorporate visualization into your training regimen. The choice ultimately rests with you. Mindset Matters Athletics advocates adopting visualization as a fundamental aspect of athletic training as it can have transformative effects on athletic achievement.

Visualization is a powerful mental tool that can help athletes enhance their performance, manage stress, and improve their mental health. Its transformative potential is worth exploring and incorporating into your training regimen.

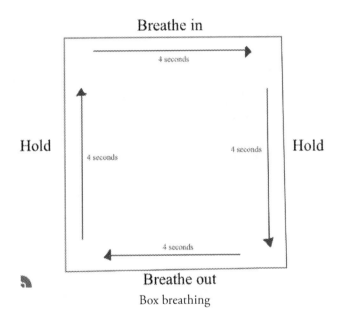

Box breathing

FIELD NOTES

Visualization

- Creates a Visual Blueprint for Success
- Improves Personal Performance
- Builds Confidence through Mental Repetitions
- Supplements Traditional Training Routines
- See it First in Your Mind and Then on the Field
- Helps Manage Adversity and Stress
- Helps Slow Things Down because you Have Seen it Already
- Box Breathing 4x4x4x4

CAMP
FIVE

ATTITUDE

Coach Davis, former MLB Manager Chris Woodward, Coach Mason

Maintaining a positive attitude is essential in sports as it helps athletes stay optimistic and constructive even in challenging situations. For instance, a player who encourages teammates and looks for opportunities to turn the game around despite the team's losing score can inspire their peers and enhance their performance. A positive attitude helps athletes bounce back from setbacks, learn from their mistakes, and maintain a growth mindset.

A study published in the Journal of Sports Sciences found, "A positive attitude is a crucial factor in athletes' success. Athletes with a positive attitude are likelier to persist in facing challenges, maintain their motivation, and perform better under pressure." (Jones, M. V., Lane, A. M., Bray, S. R., Uphill, M., & Catlin, J. (2011).

A gratitude attitude is a positive approach that can make a significant difference in achieving success. A positive attitude in sports influences mental and physical performance, emotional health, and relationships with teammates, coaches, friends, and family.

A positive attitude brings light, hope, and enthusiasm to life, creating an environment that fosters success. The impact of a positive attitude is not limited to sports but extends to all aspects of life. It helps individuals achieve their goals, succeed, and increase overall happiness. It also boosts energy levels, provides inner peace and strength, and improves the ability to deal with adversity or difficulties.

Maintaining a positive attitude helps athletes achieve better mental and physical health, reduced stress, improved self-confidence, enhanced brain function, and longer life expectancy. A positive attitude in sports also fosters positive social interactions, leading to fulfilling relationships and a prosperous social life.

Having a positive attitude is crucial in many aspects of life. It can inspire and motivate us and those around us, creating a positive ripple effect. In addition, it contributes to better performance in sports and other areas by fostering focus, resilience, and a can-do mindset. Cultivating a positive attitude opens us up to new possibilities, attracts positive experiences, and creates a supportive environment for success. It's important to remember that our attitude is a choice, and by choosing positivity and gratitude, we can transform our lives and positively impact others.

We can attract good people and great opportunities by consistently viewing things positively. People are naturally drawn to those who are friendly, likable, and trustworthy, and having a positive attitude can help us embody these qualities. This can lead to good things on the horizon and a life filled with gratitude.

The Bible provides us multiple examples that encourage us to focus on positive and constructive thoughts. Here is one great example: - Philippians 4:8: "Finally, brothers and sisters, whatever is true, whatever is noble, whatever is right, whatever is pure, whatever is lovely, whatever is admirable— if anything is excellent or praiseworthy—think about such things." This passage encourages us to focus on positive and uplifting thoughts rather than dwelling on negative ones.

Athletes who embody a positive attitude have successfully succeeded in their respective sports. Today, we will discuss some of the most recognized athletes and observe how having a positive attitude has impacted their success and propelled them to the top of their respective sports.

Many athletes have discussed the importance of a positive mindset when playing sports. One example is Tim Tebow, a former American football quarterback and professional baseball outfielder. Tebow has spoken extensively about his faith and how it has helped him maintain a positive mindset throughout his athletic career. He has said: "For me, it's having an attitude of gratitude and understanding that every day is a gift. It's about having a positive outlook and not letting circumstances dictate your joy or your attitude." - Tim Tebow. This quote highlights how Tebow believes that a positive mindset is essential to success in sports and that his faith has helped him stay focused and motivated even in challenging situations.

Stephen Curry is a devout Christian who has spoken publicly about his faith numerous times. Here is one of his quotes about his faith: "I know why I play the game, and it's not to score 30 points a night, but to use the stage I'm on. I've been put here for a specific purpose: to be a witness and share my testimony as I go through it." - Stephen Curry. This quote demonstrates how Curry sees his basketball career as a platform to share his faith and positively influence others.

Another example is Allyson Felix, an American track and field sprinter and Olympic gold medalist. Felix has spoken about how her faith has helped her maintain a sense of gratitude and perspective throughout her athletic career. She has said: "I try to approach everything with a spirit of gratitude. Acknowledging the good you already have in your life is the foundation for all abundance." - Allyson Felix. This quote highlights how Felix believes that gratitude is a crucial component of success in sports and life. By appreciating what she has and focusing on the positive, Felix can maintain a sense of perspective and stay motivated even in challenging situations.

Pat Summitt, Legendary Tennessee Women's Basketball Coach, emphasized having a positive mindset, believing in oneself, and finding the good in every situation. Her approach led to on-court success and inspired and empowered her players to become their best selves. Pat Summit was a devout Christian. She was known for her strong faith and credited her faith as one of the key factors that helped her throughout her life and career. Summit was a Sevier Heights

Baptist Church member in Knoxville, Tennessee, where she was actively involved in various ministries. She often spoke publicly about her faith and how it impacted her life and career.

These athletes/coaches demonstrate how a positive attitude can fuel success, inspire others, and help navigate challenges effectively. Their stories inspire athletes and individuals in various areas of life, reminding us of the power of positivity and gratitude in achieving our goals.

Gratitude Exercise

Taking time to acknowledge things you are grateful for can boost your mood. We tend to take things for granted missing opportunities to get psyched up about all the blessings we have. Make a gratitude list based on each letter of the alphabet. If you can't think of one for every letter, don't worry. The goal is to get yourself to pay attention to the good. It's not about completing this exercise.

Some Suggestions: Consider . . . things, people, places, events, activities. Think about your spiritual, physical, emotional, social, physical aspects.

I'M GRATEFUL FOR...
A
B
C
D
E
F
G
H
I
J
K
L
M
N
O
P
Q
R
S
T
U
V
W
X
Y
Z

Gratitude Worksheet

FIELD NOTES

Attitude

- Positive Attitude is a Critical Factor in Determining Levels of Success
- Positive Attitude Improves Physical Perormance
- Positive Attitude Improves Mental Health
- Positive Attitude Improves Relationships with Teamates, Coaches, Friends and Family
- Positive Attitude Reduces Stress
- Positive Attitude Improves Brain Function
- Positive Attitude Attracts Quality People
- Positive Attitude Creates Opportunities and Opens Doors
- Positive Attitude Improves your Life and the Lives of Everyone Around You
- Positive Attitude is Contagious

CAMP
SIX

TRAIN

An example of sports routines and habits of excellence is when athletes consistently practice and refine their skills on and off the field. For instance, a basketball player may have a daily routine of shooting practice, weight training, and reviewing game footage to identify areas for improvement. They may also have habits of excellence, such as maintaining a healthy diet, getting enough sleep, and staying hydrated, which can improve their performance and reduce the risk of injury. By establishing routines and habits of excellence, the athlete is more likely to develop a strong work ethic, discipline, and focus, which can lead to better performance and outcomes in the long run.

MMA Athlete
Volleyball

A study published in the International Journal of Sports Physiology and Performance found that "The training process is a critical determinant of athletic success. Athletes who engage in a well-designed training process emphasizing progressive overload, periodization, and individualization are likelier to achieve their goals and maximize their performance potential." (Issurin, V. (2013).

Habits and routines are crucial in determining our success and level of excellence. They define our identity, values, and priorities. As Steven Covey emphasizes, our habits can either make or break us. We become the result of what we repeatedly do.

Our habits shape our identity and communicate our values and priorities to those around us. Lewis Howes, a former College All-American and N.F.L. player, asserts that champions aren't born but created when we embrace and commit to life-changing positive habits.

Our daily actions, weekly routines, monthly commitments, and yearly consistency shape us. Whether we reach our full potential or fall short is directly influenced by our habits. The accumulation of small actions performed consistently over time yields substantial results rather than sporadic bursts of motivation.

James Clear's *Atomic Habits* book delves into the power of habits and how they can either help or hinder us. Clear suggests that our success is not determined by our goals alone but by the systems we have in place—the methods that are shaped by our habits. He states, "You do not rise to the level of your goals; you fall to the level of your systems." The systems created by our habits generate gradual, incremental improvements and make all the difference.

To be the best version of ourselves, we must assess our habits and ask ourselves whether they are helping or hindering our progress. Trevor Moawad advises taking the element of choice out of the equation if we genuinely desire to be the best. It is about recognizing that achieving greatness takes what it takes—it requires unwavering commitment.

Identifying which habits are beneficial and reinforcing them is vital. Similarly, recognizing which habits are detrimental and eliminating them is essential. As Brian Johnson suggests, we increase our chances of success by removing the option or choice from the equation. Doing something 99% of the time may be challenging but doing it 100% becomes effortless when it becomes a firm decision rather than a wavering choice.

Changing and establishing habits requires a systematic approach. It necessitates a plan and deliberate effort to create patterns that align with our goals and aspirations. By implementing a well-designed system, we can effectively cultivate habits and routines that contribute to our journey of excellence.

To overcome obstacles and reach our full potential, we must create a system that includes habits of excellence. The small, consistent actions we take day in, and day out add up to significant progress. Success lies in evaluating our habits, assessing the effectiveness of our current systems, and adopting habits that have led to others' success. By identifying habits that contribute positively to our goals and eliminating those that don't, we can create a well-designed system that nurtures and grows our traditions of excellence.

The MMA ELEVATE program prioritizes habits and routines that promote excellence. By replacing detrimental habits with empowering ones, we stay on the path towards achieving our goals. A well-structured system or routine provides the strength to adhere to the plan, even when faced with challenges to self-control and discipline. It is crucial for our system and our underlying motivation to be stronger than our fleeting feelings, especially on days when we lack motivation.

As we progress in our athletic journey, the talent levels among top competitors eventually plateau. The distinguishing factor between these athletes lies in their developed systems and mindset to navigate the ups and downs. The ability to handle rough waters and the inevitable hardships requires the power of habits and routines of excellence.

Habits are not just small actions but the building blocks of our lives. They can shape our character, determine our success, and define who we become. Understanding how habits work and harnessing their power is essential for personal growth and achieving excellence. Let's take a closer look at the ice cube analogy.

An ice cube at 25 degrees remains unchanged; it maintains its form and properties. The ice cube persists even if the temperature rises slightly to 28 or 32 degrees. However, change starts when the temperature increases by just one degree, from 32 to 33 degrees. This small change may seem insignificant initially, but it marks the beginning of a transformation.

As the temperature rises incrementally, the ice cube begins to melt. The change may be slow at first, but as the temperature climbs higher and higher, the ice cube melts rapidly. It is the consistent and gradual increase in temperature that eventually brings about significant change.

Similarly, in our lives, small changes over time have the

power to transform us from who we are today into who we aspire to be tomorrow. The key is to make the right changes, engage in the proper habits, and consistently work towards our goals.

Now, let's explore the example of a plane journey from Los Angeles to New York City. The pilots set off on their flight with seemingly accurate coordinates and plans. However, they miscalculate the direction they are flying by just 3.5 degrees. At first, this deviation might not appear significant. Still, as the plane continues its journey, hour after hour, the pilots' routines and habits based on their incorrect coordinates lead them astray. Despite their routine checks indicating they are on course, the pilots find themselves hundreds of miles off-course in Washington, DC. The initial misalignment of just 3.5 degrees compounds over time, significantly deviating from their intended destination. This example highlights the importance of setting precise coordinates and directions.

Suppose we need to be more intentional about our habits and routines. In that case, even slight deviations can lead us far from our desired goals. It is crucial to know exactly where we want to go, reverse engineer the path to get there, and start acting today. To understand how habits work and build an effective system, we need to examine how habits are formed. Charles Duhigg, in his book "The Power of Habit," presents the habit loop, which consists of three components: a trigger or cue, a routine or action, and a reward.

Let's apply this concept to our goal of achieving excellent physical condition. We recognize that our previous workout and nutrition habits were not serving us well, so we replaced them with new, positive habits. First, we implement a habit-stacking approach, aiming to stack wins on top of wins throughout our day. Instead of hitting the snooze button multiple times in the morning, we consciously get up as soon as the alarm goes off. This becomes our first win of the day, serving as the trigger or cue for our habit loop.

We gain an extra 30 minutes each morning by resisting the temptation to sleep. This time becomes an opportunity to invest in ourselves and engage in activities contributing to our physical well-being. We then proceed to make our bed, following the advice of Admiral McRaven, who famously stated that starting the day with a small win, such as making your bed, sets the tone for success. Next, we wear our workout clothes and go for a 20-minute run, incorporating physical activity into our routine. This action becomes essential to our habit loop, aligning with our goal of achieving excellent physical condition.

Concentration grids are a great way to train your focus. See the concentration grid below for an example. Recommend trying out www.concentrationgrids.com to keep track of your history.

36	68	38	12	60	29	13	79	08	90
46	18	67	95	44	87	06	69	41	61
84	63	89	50	37	62	47	77	74	09
51	83	78	55	05	73	64	31	49	91
80	96	10	52	72	24	53	43	27	94
22	16	25	00	58	45	28	71	03	40
19	66	32	81	85	23	93	20	02	70
26	76	92	14	17	07	21	01	99	98
04	54	86	82	39	48	65	57	88	11
33	34	42	75	97	35	15	30	56	59

You can always print off new concentration grids, or perform these exercises online at: ConcentrationGrids.com

Concentration Grids

FIELD NOTES

Train

- Habits and Routines Directly Determine Success Levels
- Habits Make or Break Us
- Habits abd Routines Shape Who We are and Show Everyone What We Value
- Habits and Routines Completed 100% of the Time are Easy and Become Our Norm
- Habits and Routines Done Over Time Create Massive Change
- Habits and Routines of Excellence Separate Athletes as Physical Talent Evens Out
- Habits and Routines are Essential Building Blocks of Our Lives

CAMP
SEVEN

EVALUATE

An example in sports of evaluating your performance to be better moving forward is when an athlete reviews their performance after a competition or game to identify areas for improvement. For instance, a swimmer who doesn't perform as well as they hoped in a race may review their split times, analyze their technique, and identify areas for improvement in their training regimen. They may also seek feedback from their coach or teammates to gain different perspectives and insights. By evaluating their performance, the athlete can identify specific areas for improvement, set new goals, and adjust their training accordingly. This approach can help athletes stay motivated and focused and continuously improve their skills and performance.

A study published in the Journal of Sport and Exercise Psychology found that "Evaluation is a critical component of the performance improvement process in sports. Athletes who regularly self-evaluate or receive feedback from coaches or peers are more likely to identify areas for improvement, set goals, and progress towards achieving those goals." (Myers, N. D., & Feltz, D. L. (2008).

As we progress through our ELEVATE program, we must ensure that we are on the right track and making the desired progress. To do this, we start by measuring and evaluating everything we do. Measuring and evaluating our progress allows us to take the right actions at the right time for the desired outcomes. Therefore, we need to track where we start, where we are, and how close we are to where we want to be.

To track our performance, we need to keep a notebook where we document and monitor our physical performance levels. We should also ensure our training aligns with our intended trajectory. We must measure and evaluate our progress in every area of our life that we wish to improve, such as the weight room, classroom, and other areas.

In each camp of our ELEVATE program, we can find ways to measure our performance in each area. For instance, we can evaluate our Elite Mindset using Carol Dweck's Growth vs. Fixed Mindset assessment tool to determine our current levels of growth or Elite Mindset abilities as we begin our mental performance training. We can also use this tool periodically to assess our progress.

We implement the "Well, Better, How" routine every week to evaluate our systems and progress. On Sundays, we reflect on our week and what went well. We also identified improvement areas and developed a plan to make it happen. We continue doing the things that align with our goals and list our above-the-line and below-the-line behaviors for the week. Above-the-line behaviors are those that benefit us, while below-the-line behaviors are those that hinder us.

We list things we did not do well and need to improve, such as eating well, being punctual, staying focused, or managing screen time. We then write down how we plan to address these areas of improvement—for example, packing lunch to eat better, preparing our practice jersey in advance, maintaining eye contact with coaches, or setting screen time limits. The "Well, Better, How" routine keeps us focused on what's essential and reduces the time it takes to reach our goals.

Furthermore, we need to evaluate our Inner Circle, which is one of the most critical areas of our lives. We must look closely at the five people we spend the most time with, excluding family members. We must assess their value to our lives and whether they help us become the person we want to be. Applying the Law of Sacrifice, we may need to make tough decisions about who truly supports and adds value to our lives. Finding individuals who support us and add value to our lives can be challenging. Still, it's our responsibility to seek them out. We must move on from friends and teammates who create distractions, display jealousy, or hinder our success. We must protect the circle of people we trust, who want the best for us and will support us in reaching our goals.

It is vital to surround yourself with individuals who excel in the areas where you want to improve. Observe and learn from them. Seek out people who share your mindset, drive, determination, and goals. Being around people who inspire you will help motivate you to push yourself to new heights.

Evaluate your mission statement regularly. It is the guiding force behind your actions and decisions. Ask yourself if it still aligns with your current goals and needs adjustment. Life is unpredictable, and we must be prepared to adapt and overcome it. Sometimes, we must change our approach and adjust to stay on track. Embrace these changes, learn from them, and strive to become better. Your ability to handle setbacks and adversity will help you use them to your advantage.

Your 14.24 represents 1% of your day, so it is crucial to be intentional about how you use it. Plan how to use those 14 minutes and 24 seconds each day to improve yourself. It could be reading, exercising, meditating, or anything that aligns with your goals. Similarly, evaluate your 168 schedule to ensure you are intentional about your time. Make sure that you are not allowing others to dictate your schedule. Remember that time is your most precious resource, so guard it wisely.

FIELD NOTES

Evaluate

- Constant Evaluation is a Critical Component of Improved Success, Performance and Progress
- Constant Evalauation Allows Continuous Allignment with Goals
- Evaluations Should Include a Well, Better, How Exercise
- Evaluations Include Constant Review of Your Inner Circle of Trust
- Evaluations Include Constant Review of Time Management and Organization (168/14.24)
- Evaluations Expose Needed Corrective Measures

CONCLUSION

If you want to be mentally tough, follow the ELEVATE program. Be process-driven and not outcome-driven. Have systems in place because the road to greatness is narrow, but it is a choice. Keep this book in your game bag and reference it whenever needed. ELEVATE your game! Your investment in yourself will yield lifelong benefits. You can perform in any environment and succeed with the tools and processes you've learned. You will open doors and seize opportunities by continuing to utilize these skills, strategies, and techniques. You will become a mentally tough, resilient athlete and individual who not only deals with adversity but also leverages it to your advantage.

At Mindset Matters Athletics, we sincerely thank you for entrusting us to help you prepare, perform, and train your mental game. We appreciate that you chose us to assist you on your journey toward becoming the best version of yourself. Keep pushing, breaking down barriers, and working toward your dreams and goals. Don't let anything or anyone stand in your way. Own everything in your life and attack! Remember, train your brain to ELEVATE your game!!

In memory of Austin Daniel Davis "Cherish the
moments that create memories to last a lifetime"

ACKNOWLEDGMENTS

All glory and praise to God, without you nothing is possible. Through all the trials, triumphs, and tragedies you will never leave us.

BIBLIOGRAPHY

Cumming, J., & Ramsey, R. (2009). Imagery interventions in sport. Journal of Imagery Research in Sport and Physical Activity, 4(1), 1-23. doi: 10.2202/1932-0191.1046.

Gould, D., Dieffenbach, K., & Moffett, A. (2002). Psychological characteristics and their development in Olympic champions. Journal of Applied Sport Psychology, 14(3), 172-204. doi: 10.1080/10413200290103509

Kleiber, D. A., & Brock, S. J. (1992). The effects of goal setting on swimming performance: A replication and extension. Journal of Sport and Exercise Psychology, 14(4), 347-359.

Tod, D., Thatcher, R., & Rahman, R. (2015). Implications of extreme ownership for developing mental toughness and training resilience in sport. Journal of Human Kinetics, 47(1), 155-167. doi: 10.1515/hukin-2015-0043)

Jones, M. V., Lane, A. M., Bray, S. R., Uphill, M., & Catlin, J. (2011). Development and validation of the Sport Attributional Style Scale. Journal of Sports Sciences, 29(12), 1299-1311. doi: 10.1080/02640414.2011.587652)

Issurin, V. (2013). New horizons for the methodology and physiology of training periodization. International Journal of Sports Physiology and Performance, 8(4), 327-334. doi: 10.1123/ijspp.8.4.327

Myers, N. D., & Feltz, D. L. (2008). Self-efficacy, evaluation, and goal-setting in collegiate track and field athletes. Journal of Sport and Exercise Psychology, 30(1), 75-87. doi: 10.1123/jsep.30.1.75

Jordan, M., & Fine, M. (2005). Driven from within. Simon and Schuster.

Hamm, M., & Heifetz, A. (2000). Go for the goal: A champion's guide to winning in soccer and life. HarperCollins.

Jackson, P., & Delehanty, H. (2013). Eleven rings: The soul of success. Penguin.

Bible. (n.d.). Galatians 6:5. In Holy Bible (New International Version). S.P.: Biblica.

Philippians 4:8. (n.d.). In Holy Bible (New International Version). S.P.: Biblica.

ABOUT THE COACHES

Coach Davis   Coach Dennis

Coaches
Meet the Coaches of Mindset Matters Athletics

Meet Coach Chad Dennis and Coach Dan Davis - two highly accomplished individuals dedicated to helping athletes succeed. With their extensive experience in leadership and training, they have developed a program called ELEVATE, designed to help athletes build a strong foundation for success in sports and life.

Coach Dennis has spent many years working in law enforcement. He is a former NCAA D1 baseball player for Eastern Kentucky University. He has also coached high-level athletic teams for over 25 years. He has a proven record of creating high-performance athletes, teams, and coaches. He understands what it takes to get athletes to the next level and has worked with hundreds of successful athletes on their mental performance.

Coach Davis is a retired Sergeant Major from the U.S. Army who has operated and led teams in some of the most demanding, diverse, and challenging environments. As a former collegiate baseball player, he was selected to play for the All-Army Sports program for several years. He was chosen as head coach of the program in 2019. He currently coaches at the collegiate level and understands the importance of controlling the chaos during high-pressure situations. Coach Davis has worked with hundreds of athletes, assisting them in elevating their mental performance in their chosen sport.

Coach Dennis and Coach Davis deeply understand the importance of mental performance in athletics and life. They have studied, worked with, and trained alongside some of the most successful people on the planet. With ELEVATE, they aim to help athletes set a solid foundation for success, drawing upon their own experiences in leadership and athletic achievement.

Contact Information: www.mindsetmattersathletics.com

Coaches together

Printed in the United States
by Baker & Taylor Publisher Services